Woman in Winter

Eve Pearce

Hearing Eye

HEARING EYE
TORRIANO MEETING HOUSE
POETRY PAMPHLET SERIES No. 52

Hearing Eye
Box 1, 99 Torriano Avenue
London NW5 2RX, UK
email: books@hearingeye.org
www.hearingeye.org

ISBN: 978-1-905082-29-2

Acknowledgements
Some of the poems in this collection first appeared in the following
publications; 'Stepmother' in *Images of Women* (Second Light
Network/Arrowhead Press, 2006), 'The English Lesson' in *RADA* magazine
(Issue 29, 2005), 'Whose Child?' in *The Morning Star*, 'Asylum Seeker' in
Poetry on the Lake (Stranger/Wyvern Works, 2006).
'Birthright' was a runner-up in the Yorkshire Open Poetry Competition, 2006.

I would like to thank Katherine Gallagher, John Rety and Susan Johns for
much help. – EP

Printed by Catford Print Centre

Cover image and design by Martin Parker

Contents

Rain 5

Legacy 6

Birthright 8

Snowdrops 9

Cocoon 10

Man and Dog 11

Stepmother 12

Polyphotos 13

The English Lesson 15

For Esmé 17

Family Portrait 18

In the Park 20

Sachertorte 21

Whose child? 22

Asylum Seeker 23

Three o'clock in the Afternoon 24

Blues in the Night 25

The Man in the Cart 26

Meeting 28

Sonnet for Dead Friends 30

Waning Moon 31

Hebridean Air 32

Rainbow 34

Woman in Winter .35

For Alan, Emma & Faith

Rain

It rained in the night.
My eyes opened to strings of pearls
sliding down the window
lit by the shimmer of London –
glittering backdrop to
a night-time scenario playing solely
to insomniacs and sleepwalkers.
My eyes close – still raining.

Next morning a grey wash over the city –
St. Paul's barely visible.
I think of other rainy days:
my mother's funeral –
February rain swithering 'tween sleet and snow,
Dreichit, the aunts agreed.

April rain which fell all day
as our first daughter prepared to enter
the world, from the faint stirrings of pain
at dawn (when the cat came and lay by me),
to the triumph of birth in the evening –
rain still falling.

Legacy

for Phyllida

It must have felt a very long way
for her to come back alone,
the child heavy in her womb,
leaving behind beloved husband Jack,
knowing he'd be messing about with cars
in the morning, billiards after noon,
and as sun slowly sank into azure sea
(Matisse made manifest), the Englishman's
charm would be laid on in Harry's Bar
for the edification of the demoiselles.

It must have mattered madly
that her bairn should be true Scots-born.

Her legacy – trees, skies, mountains of this land –
the copper beech, the silver birch,
and Burns' bonny rowan tree –
these have meant much to me.
As well her Bible – tissue thin pages
gold-tipped, faint scent of eau-de-cologne,
an inscription in her beautiful hand,
I will lift up mine eyes unto the hills.

She died when I was seven.
I remember her face on the pillow,
colourless as drifts of snow
outwith the hospital gates –

not much more. Only that when I turned
to wave goodbye she didn't see me,
had eyes for him alone.

Her legacy's been worth the telling, worth the pain,
for I have seen sunlight strike Dunottar's ruins
through curtains of rain, and wild sea-sprayed branches
cliff-high, glimpsed from a train have enlaced me
with ancient magic.

We are the things we love.

Birthright

Aberdeen! Jute Street – fifty-five. *Aye, right.*
Are granite slabs still split in mason's yard? BOOM!
the giant hammer swings. I shiver with delight.

Memorials for Aberdonians, angel-bright
marble monuments defying endless doom.
Fifty-five Jute Street – here y'are, and I alight.

Back green – iron stair. I'm six, leap the last flight
to suck on rusty fleur-de-lys, taste of the tomb
floods my mouth now. I shiver with delight.

Patterned lino on inside stair – no light
but on heavy door brass plate gleams through gloom.
Fifty-five Jute Street, Aberdeen – this night.

Granny's speciality was the bear-hug *Tight.*
Brawny arms surround me. Safe as in the womb
I gasp for air and shiver with delight.

It's why I came. In cold North-Eastern light
would memories, sae lang syne still bloom?
Fifty-five Jute Street Aberdeen is my birthright.
I was born here. I shiver with delight.

Snowdrops

Like the wolf in a fairy tale, biting cold
snatches at my throat as I twist the brass knob,
push the heavy door. I close it quickly,
lest my aunties hear (They've gone for *a wee lie down*).

The silence of death is in this room: Grandad's parlour,
used only for weddings, christenings and at Hogmanay.
The coffin is an alien.

Luminous light filters through drawn blinds,
snow lending opal bloom to parlour tomb.
In the polished box with gleaming handles
lies my mother.
I stand on tiptoe to see her:
white shroud pin-tucked at foot,
pearl-buttoned from waist to frilled neck,
hands crossed on breast. The air has stopped.
I've seen her, but I don't believe – I have to touch;
and so like Thomas, fearful and doubting
I lay my olive hand on her ivory fingers.
                                        Icy.

In the forenoon I brave the slush on iron stairs,
pick snowdrops from the back green,
wrap their stems in silver paper,
find my father, gaunt, lost – give them to him.
For Mummy – to take with her – in her hands, I say.
He nods, pauses and walks away.

I notice the hole in the sole of his shoe.

Cocoon

Numbing, freezing, this December day;
breath visible in the foggy air
tastes metallic on the tongue.

She's close to me today – my childhood self –
thin seven year old struggling with scratchy socks,
garters so tight they leave a livid band
of skeleton white below the knee.
Swollen fingers squeeze shiny chilblained toes,
purple and itchy, into harsh brown brogues.

Today I'm seeing her plain –
brown eyes like almonds, straggly fringe,
a wee thing in her too large prickly coat
made by Granny overnight and black as the grate.

Safe in my grown-up bed I still
can hear the treadle's song:
wha'll care fir ye noo yer mammy's deed,
wha'll care fir the mitherless quine?

On February mornings, on her way to school
she's capturing snowflakes, white lozenges
on her tongue: standing still, head tipped back,
great flakes falling on eyes and lashes,
nose and lips – a world of snow
swirling and spiralling about her
as she prepares to enter her silent cocoon –
black changing so slowly to white.

NB: 'Quine' is the word for a girl child in Aberdeenshire

Man and Dog

In my memory he always whistles to the dog –
every morning a long low whistle
meant only for her, and she knows it.
At the end of the back green he climbs
the weathered mildewed fence, the bitch waiting,
never taking her eyes off him till he gives
the signal, then flying over herself,
body extended like an acrobat's –
racing ahead of him along the single goods track
pebbled with shale and fringed with swaying grass
so tall that when I squint through mossy planks
I see only parts of them – black and white fan
of Fluffy's tail, Grandad's rusty trilby.
My thin child's body ached with longing then
and does so still, when I remember how
for one perfect moment the world came together,
man and dog, railway track, grasses and sky –
her leap seemingly held in the air forever.

Stepmother

She was very small,
she always wore black,
she was not in mourning
for her life or anybody else's.
And I loved her.

Straight of back, elegant of foot,
a tiny wildcat fearing nothing;
offering the startled burglar a cup of tea,
though white hot Irish temper flared
alarmingly at cruel words or deeds.

She was a champion of pitiful things –
bones begged from the butcher
for a one-eyed, mangy mutt,
smelly sprats boiled up for the alley cat,
and the child that was me rescued
from festering boredom in a cold city –
shown a world undreamed of:
London seen through pillars of white,
lime juice and cheese straws to eat,
a soft divan to sleep on.

Most mornings, even now, fifty years on
I wake expecting her for breakfast:
coffee, croissants, cherry jam –
till I remember with a tiny pang
she left me years ago.

Polyphotos

Taken soon after I arrived in London –
one polyphoto from a sheet – thirty
I think – an inch square, in black and white –
this the sole survivor.
I was twelve and longed to see the new me!

Pat, indulgent with the waif she'd acquired
along with a husband – said Selfridges
was the place, so we walked down Edgware Road
and I was immortalised on Selfridge Lower Ground.
It was 1941.

Here I am, biting my lip slightly,
but happy with my sprigged blouse,
my brown skirt with straps – height of fashion –
ribbon (I think it was red) a bit skew-whiff
in my hair, my dark eyes full of hope.

Polyphotos had conquered Europe too
it seems, in the midst of other conquests –
your Diary has a page of snaps
and there you are, an Amsterdam version,
looking up at me, dressed not unlike,
with your black hair, your beautiful dark eyes.
The year is 1941.

My heart judders, as the trains must have.

I've always known: we could have changed places.

Only seven weeks separate us.
Look at us – expectancy in our faces.
We are like two stretches of smooth sand
the tide has not yet reached.
When it does, you will be swept away.
I remain safe for sixty years.

Brave my sister, stay a little longer,
and when I need it, hold out your hand
and help me through the dark.

The English Lesson

A hand held up, a hand with a small hole:
the autumn sun, dying like mighty Caesar
shines through – halo of gold on pallid palm.

A small man, Mr Maltby, suited in rusty navy,
striped shirt with collar not so much frayed
as chewed. *This afternoon*, he says – *Shakespeare*.

A sort of sigh goes up – the dusty air
charged with anticipation. Of what?
Today, he says, *I give you Anthony*.
And he holds up his hand.

Friends Romans Countrymen –
No need to ask us *lend our ears*, or eyes,
that one translucent spot everyone's focus.
Then I remember, cornered at playtime,
being told – *bullet went straight thru 'is 'and,*
'e told us once – 'strue – 'e said it wor
a place called Passion Dale.

So Shakespeare's murdered Julius
fell for us on Flanders Fields, and in light
of setting sun Caesar's corpse was strewn
with blood-red poppies.

Now Mr Maltby becomes the noble Roman,
no longer bald but crowned with laurel,
a full length robe – the toga suited him –

best of all the small hole in his right palm
convinced us that he had seen War,
Betrayal, Death, and earned his right to move us
with Shakespeare's words – we, the unlikely mob
at Caesar's funeral.

For Esmé

Pear tree blossoms shimmer white,
sighing against pillars on a terrace –
the loggia, whispers my mistress guide.
Loggia, I repeat, the word sweet as apricots
in my mouth. Music pours from the Hall –
Smetana – *My Homeland*, she murmurs –
My Homeland I nod trance-like,
dappled sun falling on rows
of angels in blue uniforms.
My new school!

Great windows billow light, the music
a vortex, a coil entwining me –
and, told to shush and creep along a row
to empty place – new, late and shy –
of course I stumble.

She looked up then, amusement was it
in her glance? Whilst I, recovering balance,
fell headlong for two fair plaits and one
raised eyebrow, sliding onto sun-warmed chair
heard her mutter, staring straight ahead:
La di da, di da. Fools the lot of them!

Love swelled like Smetana's river,
dancing, chancing, romancing,
the shining current carried us along –
childhood left on the shore like a caul.

Family Portrait

Grandad, you're pickled in aspic –
I can't get through to you.

Sae lang since, a hundred years lang syne
you sat for the family portrait,
you and Stewart and Granny – mine,
but one I never knew, though having her look
(or so it was said) when I was a quine.

Fine she still sits in her velvet black,
wee lassie on her knee,
angled away, lost in thought, a knack
you laughed at – aye a dreamer she.
Two years, two more bairns before she's laid
in lonely grave.

Aged two, my Auntie Elsie, heather-filled basket
dangling from tiny fist, frowns at a world
which soon will leave her crippled, a misfit.
Bored nursemaid, steep brae, pram overturns –
bonny blue-eyed lass, white dress, blue sash,
rendered into the fearsome maiden aunt I knew.

You're pickled in aspic Grandad
as you pose in your Sunday best
your braw wee lad perched on velvet chair,
in his hands a tall wooden ship, and lest
he will not part with it, cannot bear,
you let him ken – in your gentle voice:

It's nay yours, Stewart, just haud it for noo.
So he gives it back to the photo-man
when the last flash dies, just as he would one day
fight in Flanders, in his unquestioning, obedient way.

My Uncle Stewart, who one fine morn,
having delivered the daily milk to Maryhill
let himself in, noticing his sock was torn,
leaving his Wellingtons like sentinels
outwith the door – saw the water how
it sparkled, filling the green enamel bowl –
socks off, and careful not to spill now
on gleaming lino, stepped in, sole
arbiter at last of his own destiny – his life –
holding a chrome electric one-bar fire,
(bought recently to please a strong-willed wife),
leant to switch it on, and deep in the mud and mire
of Flanders – smelling the stench, hearing the guns,
finally joined his pals, a few years late –
poppies bursting in the air like scarlet suns.

In the Park

On the same bench
he sat every day,
the old man with the felt hat.

One day he wasn't there,
and in my heart
a black hole opened
where his image had been.

Sachertorte

The Blue Danube plays while I sip my coffee,
waiting for the museum to open.
I eat my sachertorte. It drips with cream.

Emperor Franz Josef looks down on me,
the only customer, sunk in my huge armchair.
Is this Vienna? No, this city is Polish.
This city is Lodz, where gypsies were rounded up
from far and wide to be massacred.
Lodz – a good Catholic city.

My coffee has a bitter taste.
The cherries on my torte are too red.

When the museum opens
the brochure tells me this town
had the second-largest ghetto in Poland;
a Jewish ghetto, so not only the gypsies.
There are photos of the Nazi era
(not many, and confined to the basement):
in one, Roma women cradling babies
in their check shawls are being herded
up the street I've just walked.

My knee, which hasn't been too good all day
is suddenly worse.

N.B. In English Lodz is pronounced as Wooj

Whose child?

Whose child is this, lying by the roadside?
Is it Arab or Israeli?
Lebanese or Iranian?
Palestinian – Iraqi?
Dead or alive?
Is it a Zionist zealot –
a member of Hezbollah?

This child has not yet learnt
there is no God but Allah.
He has no use for an eye for an eye,
a tooth for a tooth.
Whose child is this?

For unto us a child is born.

When he grows up will he attain paradise
in an instant? Will the virgins be waiting?
Meanwhile he has no mother to suckle him –
to be proud when he straps on the martyr's belt.

For unto us a son is given.
A son – is given – unto us.

Whose child is this?

Asylum Seeker

for Helen Bamber

Believe me – do you – truth I tell, she says.
Her eyes like pale stars in a dawn sky
plead. These, her first words in countless days
like electric current between us. A sigh –
hers or mine, no telling – only the pain
in her voice like static, lips open wide
coated with spume – words gurgle out. In vain
I try to catch the drift, swim with the tide –
useless – I'm drowning. Again I miss the clue –
probes – she whispers, *cattle* – and hangs her head.
I only have to listen, note it down, she's due
that – breathing, alive, when surely I'd be dead.
A wind blows round my heart. She asks again,
Believe me? Knows the answer – feels my pain.

Three o'clock in the Afternoon

From where I lie on the sofa
a triangle of ragged ochre leaves
is all I see of the mighty chestnut.
Three o'clock in the afternoon –
autumn – jagged slash of blue
piercing a pale grey sky.
Why do I think of the bull fight?
My head aches. I want to sleep.

Glare of the Southern sun,
gleaming trumpets blare,
introducing a spectacle unlike any other.
The climax approaches –
the bull roars,
the crowds sighs almost tenderly,
silence as the red cloak flutters,
the beast staggers and falls,
the matador lifts his arm, resplendent –
replacing the sun.

I seem to have slept.

Blues in the Night

I love musicians –
the way they simply pick up their instruments
and play.

Jools Holland – lovely Jools, had a very old hand on
the other night: Dr. John. Must have been
doing his thing *since Pussy was a cat.*

The Doctor wore a green felt hat
with a brighter green ribbon round it.
His suit had seen better days.
The baby grand had a strip of coarse lace
tacked on to the straight bit – a human skull
sat on top of the piano. Nobody
said a word about it. It was just there.
Memento mori with a vengeance.

Gravelly voice singing *Blues in the Night.*
I'm seven again, sitting at my cousin Freddie's feet,
and he's belting out in a Glasgow twang –
Ma mama dun tol' me, when I was in knee-pants,
Ma mama dun tol' me, son – a woman's
a two-faced, a worrisome thing
that leads you to sing
those Blues in the Night.

We got *That Old Black Magic* after that.

I love musicians.

The Man in the Cart

A September afternoon on Teesside,
that narrow industrial strip –
smell of sulphur hangs in the air,
fiery plumes erupt like flaming swords
in a metallic sky, the light is eerie.
Alone in my mini I'm lost –
I could be in Hell.
The road winds up a hill – I crest it
and see him instantly far below,
the man in the cart –

a huge man with flowing black hair
and horse to match, standing up, driving his beast
hell for leather across a forlorn sandpit.
Not a soul around but him and me –
and him leaning back against the wind,
baring his teeth, his hair streaming,
for all the world like an illustration
from the Tales of the Brothers Grimm.

For years I told the story nobody believed,
asked people – did you ever see? Hear?
They'd shake their heads, incredulous.

One Sunday, cover of the Supplement – there he was:
black boots, red scarf, beautiful hair streaming
in the wind, just as I'd seen him from above.
They'd held an annual race for centuries,
Romanies – fewer every year.

One of these days I'll try to find that road.
My man'll be old now – but it comes to me
that in one of the photos there was a lad –
a lad with long black hair, holding the horse.

Meeting

Cradle me within your arm,
touch my breast,
keep me from all hidden harm,
lay the past to rest.

Grey November afternoon seeps sullenly indoors,
questions taut as cobwebs hang in the air.
Panic like a too-tight scarf sears her throat.
Shall we have tea, he says at last –
Earl Grey, Darjeeling, Lapsang Souchong, yes?
She smiles. *Darjeeling please* –
hold fast to tea-time's honoured ritual,
by millions sanctified each day at four or five,
keeping the spiders in their webs,
the big cats in their lairs.

Where did it go – the grief, the pain?
Does her arthritic finger hold it now,
or his slight limp?

Outside the Northern rain streams down and feet
slip-slopping on grey pavements clop and clang.
How could you, love, return to this sad town?
She hasn't uttered. Yet he says
The city's very pleasant now, you'd scarcely know it.
No, you'd be amazed,
and of a sudden lays a finger on her arm.
She looks and it is gone, was never there perhaps,
yet blood leaps like a leopard, walls no longer still,

muscles long lain dormant heave, contract
and spiral towards the ceiling at his will.

Cradle me within your arm,
touch my breast,
keep me from all hidden harm,
lay the past to rest.

Sonnet for Dead Friends

Twenty five years since she swallowed the pills,
gulped the brandy, kicked off her scarlet mules,
waited for sun-drenched death in Beverley Hills:
long-limbed, life-loving Rachel, breaker of rules
felled by life's blows: a careless man, no child.
Then Roy – graceful, spiky, gifted, gay –
his heart gave way: Larry – warm, beguiled
by beauty, caught an eternal cold one day.
Marion, so young – Teddy, so frightened –
Glen, dearest of all – we sang to you,
hoping you heard, trusting the songs lightened
your heart, as rose sky turned to deepest blue.
They are gone – I remain. Death's a game of chance;
a leaf blowing in the wind, for them I dance.

Waning Moon

On this velvet, cloudless night
the waning moon, lopsided slice of melon
is about to fall from the sky.

Ten nights ago she rode the heavens
full and bright – a cock-horse, her Man smiling,
in control, like mine – knowing something I didn't
(and found hard to believe when he told me).

Each night she's tipped a little more,
a sliver shaved off at every appearance.
Tonight, like me, she's waiting for the final drop.

I look up.
The Man's head is turned away,
one scarcely sees the grin.

I twist my neck to catch his expression –
I'd bend over backwards if it would help.

Towards dawn I see she's fading; her Man
looking to the other side of the world
has disappeared – as will mine.

Sure enough – a shadow bending to close his suitcase
is all I glimpse in the spectral light.

Hebridean Air

In the morning I notice how
now that we're back
the skin on my arms has turned brown,
and this seems strange
when even fleeces and Fair Isle jumpers
hardly kept out the gale
which rose without warning,
like a wild cat on her hind legs –
just as we got off the ferry
and into the rattly white van,
to view the Standing Stones of Callanish.

For miles around you see them,
black against a stormy sky.
Come closer. They're granite –
silver with gleams of gold,
reflecting myriad buttercups.
I close my eyes – feel the gritty, glittering slab –
four thousand years live in my fingertips.

In Harris, daffodils still grow by the road – this in July.

We cross the Sound to Uist – tartan-carpeted lodge,
owned by a cousin of the Queen you know,
slaughtered stags adorn the walls,
one beast's head left to rot outside;
the sun goes down on luminous antlers,
skull of ivory, as dinner is served.

I am glad my arms have taken this hue,
the colour of clear burns moving swiftly
over pebbles slippery as eels:
the colour of my Celtic ancestors –

as though I'd woken up with the stigmata.

Rainbow

For you my love I shall paint a rainbow.

Red – the colour of blood, Christ's or the bull,
passion, the Magdalen's robe, the holly berry,
red – scarlet slippers by the bed.
Shade to orange – smell the blossom –
hear the Hari Krishna people,
saffron robes with orange sashes.
Hari Krishna – Hari Krishna –
cymbals distance dust and ashes.
Fields of sunflowers bend, then break and die.
Vincent's yellow chair, his golden wheat
they live for aye. Green grow the rushes o,
though slime is viridian in the stagnant pool.
Blue skies, shining on me – the Virgin's veil –
something borrowed … something …
Indigo – the Duke's tune – remember?
When I get that mood indigo.
One left – violet – the modest flower,
modesty – horrors, I see you glower –
let's call it purple – purple-stainèd mouth.

See that oil-soaked puddle by the garage door?
You could wait ages for one in the sky,
but on the ground it will always be there –
a rainbow for you, my love.

Woman in Winter

The white tulips have lost half their petals.
Star-like they shine in the gloaming,
in an empty room.
I cannot bear to say that they are dead.

Lately – since the news that is,
I seem to see with new intensity,
hear with the ears of a cat,
an unknown pulse in my finger tips
records texture, weight as never before –
the velvet of a cushion, tweed of a jacket,
soft calf of a handbag. Smells assail me.
My tastebuds are like keys on a piano,
so many sensations they pick out.

In the park the trees are leafless,
stark 'gainst sky of such a brilliant blue
it hurts my eyes. In winter's offering,
reduced, pared down, the tree lives.

Is it the same for us? Is the core left –
our essence undiminished – whatever bits
they choose to cut away?

I will believe the readiness is all.